Always more than enough!

A New Relationship
^
With Money

To: Karen
With love &
wiggles...

Happy day,

Lucy

A New Relationship
With Money

Kerry Cudmore

INTRINSIC MAGIC PRESS   Westport, MA

INTRINSIC MAGIC PRESS
PO Box N237
Westport, MA 02790

ISBN: 978-0-9915861-0-3

First edition, first printing
Printed in the United States of America

Library of Congress Control Number: 2014903693

Publisher's Cataloging-in-Publication Data

Cudmore, Kerry.

  A new relationship with money / Kerry Cudmore. – 1st ed. – Westport, MA : Intrinsic Magic Press, c2014.

    p. ; cm.

    ISBN: 978-0-9915861-0-3
    Contents: Exploration – Getting real – Moving forward.
    Summary: Introduces readers to Kerry Cudmore's Spiritual Finance perspectives and philosophy, teaching them how to change their core relationship with money to one that is fully aligned with their values.–Publisher.

    1. Finance, Personal. 2. Finance, Personal–Psychological aspects. 3. Money–Psychological aspects. 4. Self-actualization (Psychology) 5. Self-perception. 6. Self-realization. 7. Conduct of life. 8. Spiritual life. 9. Spiritual formation. I. Title.

HG179 .C83 2014   2014903693
332.024–dc23   1405

This book is dedicated to your relationship with money — a relationship that is healthy and fully aligned with your values. Even if you're not there yet, it is absolutely possible.

You can do it, and you're not alone.

Offering

I present this offering from my perspective as a coach, empowerment trainer, and firewalking instructor. I believe that we create each and every aspect of our reality, and appreciate that this can be a radical perspective. I don't expect that everything will be a fit for everybody, but I invite you to see how these perspectives fit for you.

Take what you like and leave the rest, knowing that you can return to pick up anything you left behind, whenever it suits you, in the future …

CONTENTS

Secret Suffering

When I first began changing my relationship with money, the chaos—and the debt I had accumulated—seemed insurmountable. I was sickened by what I had created out of my own ignorance and denial, and by the time I opened my eyes to the situation, I was overwhelmed. It required a lot of work to change how I related to and behaved with money. It required an act of faith to believe that the light at the end of the tunnel actually existed, even though I couldn't yet see it.

Money can be a place of secret suffering, a type of anguish that can corrode our sense of self, self-worth, relationships, careers, and even our health. It can diminish personal freedom and fulfillment. I have experienced this secret suffering personally, and it has been a long, slow journey of self-discovery, learning, and recovery.

Money is one of the last taboos in our culture. We will speak openly about sex and the intimate details of our relationships and health before we will share our secrets about money, even with the people we are closest to. The result can be terrifying and lonely; it can seem difficult, if not impossible, to connect with others and get help.

It took courage for me to confront the reality I had created, and perseverance to redefine and recreate my relationship with money. I am grateful for the progress I've made, and the tenacity it took to not be swallowed up by the process. I appreciate the bravery of every person who has shared their story with me, reminding me where I was and where my journey has taken me. Reminding me that my own secret suffering is behind me now.

I Imagine

I imagine a time when our individual and collective relationships with money are different—a time when money no longer creates stress and anxiety, no longer separates us from one another, no longer engenders discord or destruction in our relationships and within ourselves, no longer causes even one individual to suffer in silence, feeling afraid, inadequate, or ashamed.

I imagine that we stop relating to money from a perspective of insecurity and fear, choosing instead to shine a light on what has been hidden so that we can see money as it truly is: A response. A powerful teacher. An eager collaborator.

I imagine a time when our relationship with money is one that nurtures and sustains us, connecting us harmoniously to empower the individual and the collective. I imagine a time when money reaches its true potential as a vehicle for efficiently circulating resources, free of fear and dysfunction.

I imagine this future. I believe in this imagining.

Spiritual Finance:
Creating a New Relationship With Money

My Spiritual Finance journey began more than fifteen years ago. My situation was desperate, my relationship with money was broken beyond recognition, and I was faced with a choice. I could lose everything—my home, my livelihood, my relationships—or figure it out. I chose to figure it out.

The journey has been long, difficult, cathartic, and ultimately transformative. I have now learned enough to share the perspectives, techniques, and tools that I've gleaned, gathered, and invented along the way so that others don't have to navigate the long, twisting path I did. What this amounts to is a series of five classes that I call, comprehensively, Spiritual Finance. The series is designed to help people change their core relationship with money, and I have taught it to hundreds of people since

January 2008. This book explores the philosophy and perspectives, along with my own personal experiences, that have informed my creation of Spiritual Finance.

This book is not meant to replace the Spiritual Finance class series, which has value that a book alone could never replicate. It is, however, meant to provide a worthy introduction—a glimpse of what the Spiritual Finance process reveals and a first step on the path to a new relationship with money.

The book has three parts: Exploration, Getting Real, and Moving Forward. Exploration describes and explores the Spiritual Finance perspective, Getting Real defines where you are now in relation to money and traces how you got here, and Moving Forward provides specific information about how to begin your own Spiritual Finance journey.

By design, I've kept this book brief and used simple terms. The perspectives within these pages reflect a valuable retooling of how we think about and relate to money. As with any good tool, this is a book to be used again and again. It will work well now, and as you progress in your relationship with money, it will continue to yield value. What you can learn from it on your first reading will be different from what you will be able to learn later on. My hope is that what you read here will offer immediate benefits, while inviting you to visit these pages again in the future.

Part I — Exploration

Exploration

Your relationship with money is a journey that will evolve over the course of your lifetime. If you weren't aware that you've been on a journey, the process of simply opening your eyes and cultivating awareness can create major change. Any journey worth taking involves exploration into territories close and familiar or far-reaching and unknown. This is where we'll begin.

The Spiritual Finance Journey

When I teach people about changing their relationship with money, I always begin the same way: I ask them to describe money. In simple terms, and using whatever words and phrases come to mind immediately, I ask them to describe money and how they feel about it. They share things like, "It doesn't grow on trees," "I don't like it," "Here one day, gone the next," or even "I hate money." They add descriptors such as stress, worry, fear, not enough, anxiety, conflict, dirty, unattainable, unpredictable, untrustworthy, and mysterious. There is also a smattering of responses like, "It's a resource" and "It helps me do what I need to do," and words like necessity, fun (when you have it), and power. Many relate the belief that money is the root of all evil.

At this point I typically notice that the atmosphere in the room feels charged and nervous. The descriptions require effort and some degree of struggle and discomfort. I observe that my own breathing is shallow and that my palms have gotten sweaty. I ask people to notice the feeling in the room; generally, we can agree that it feels somewhat disturbed. People look uncomfortable in their seats and seem hypervigilant.

Next, I ask them to put the idea of money aside completely and describe the word "spiritual." I explain that this word, to me—and in the context that we'll use it—simply implies living according to your values, whatever those values may be. If your values are informed by a specific religious belief system, fine; if not, fine. It means living your life according to your values, however you define them. When people describe the word "spiritual," they use words such as peace, love, calm, joy, happiness, growth, connection, faith, comfort, reassurance, trust, and serenity. As people describe living life in harmony with their values, I notice that the energy in the room quickly shifts. Everyone breathes a deep sigh of relief, and people smile, calm down, and relax in their seats as the descriptions flow more easily. There's less jaggedness and more connection.

We look at the difference between these two sets of descriptions—how dissimilar they are, and how different they feel to explore. I point out that it's not just interesting what descriptions are on the lists, but what's missing as well: Anxiety and fear never show up on the spiritual list, and peace and love aren't used to describe money. This is revealing to me; it seems interesting to others as well.

I share my theory about money:

If you endeavor to live your life according to your values, and you are unable to describe money in the same way you'd describe your values, you can never have a healthy relationship with money. It cannot and will not fit with who you are as a person. Consciously or unconsciously, you'll have to keep it at a distance — or you'll be in conflict with your core beliefs. You'll be out of alignment with your values.

At this point, I notice a pause in the room; it's as if something has clicked into place and makes sense. If I could give it a voice, the pause would be saying *Hmmmm*. This is a different way to think about money, and it takes time to absorb the implications. In the pause, I notice that people are considering this new perspective.

Learning by Example

Why is it like this? How did it get this way? Why is there so much disparity between how money could serve us (as a resource in alignment with our values) and where many of us have ended up (in a place of fear, stress, and unease)? It's all related to how we learned about it.

Most of us were taught about money indirectly, as if by osmosis. From a very young age we begin to pick up on subtle and not-so-subtle messages—messages that were rarely intended to inform us about money, but nonetheless did so in powerful ways; we acquire what surrounds us, regardless of whether that reflects our values. We absorb these messages randomly, yet they become our belief system about money, without our realizing that we even have a belief system.

Consider how differently we learn about other things. The alphabet. How to wash dishes. Drive a car. Algebra. Ideally, we are directly taught by someone who already understands the concept or process, and they share their learning. Few of us learn about money this way. Consider, in contrast, how we learn the alphabet: "This is the letter A.

This is what it looks like. This is what it sounds like. This is what happens when you combine it with other letters." Few people have a destructive relationship with the alphabet, but many have a destructive relationship with money.

Ideally, as we teach our children, we teach them deliberately so that there's no confusion about the message or the information we want to convey. I did not learn about money this way; almost exclusively, I learned about it unintentionally and indirectly. I picked up my money lessons and beliefs from the people and culture that surrounded me, regardless of whether they possessed mastery of money or their beliefs reflected my values.

The people I've met who are fortunate enough to have learned about money in an intentional, direct way (and they seem to be in the minority) have different relationships with money from the one I used to have and that most people have. They possess a seemingly innate understanding and mastery that feels normal to them. This can make it difficult, if not impossible, for them to grasp what it would be like if they hadn't had this experience of direct learning; they usually don't realize that how they learned about money was different.

For me, when I reached my moment of decision—to lose it all or change things—one of my first questions was, "How did I get here?" followed quickly by "How did I learn about money?" That was the moment I became my most fascinating research project.

My exploration began with a vivid memory. I was in the fourth grade, and my parents had separated and were in the throes of a bitter divorce. At that point I only saw my dad once a week; I was extremely close to him, and looked forward to Saturdays with great anticipation. I remember waiting that day, stretching up on my tiptoes to see above the high frames of our living room windows, until I spotted my father's car pulling into the driveway and sprinted toward the door. My brother—more strategically positioned—had already raced out, and I was right behind him when my mother stopped me and said,

"Ask your father where the money is."

Every last bit of excitement and happiness drained from me; I can still remember the sickening feeling as I walked to the car and said, "Mom wants to know where the money is." He was livid. He didn't want my mother to put me in the middle like that … and he didn't have the money.

I dragged myself back to the house and told my anxious mother, "He doesn't have it." She looked angry and visibly shaken. (I know now that she must have needed that money for something important, like the mortgage, electricity, food.)

It was a devastating lesson about money. Though it only lasted a few minutes, I can feel the same sensations I had during that brief exchange—yet for most of my life, I didn't realize I had learned anything. When I began redesigning my relationship with money, however, I realized that I had learned something powerful: that money equals anxiety, anger, and suffering. I also learned that money equals conflict. Therefore, in my child's brain, it became safer to not have money.

No wonder I didn't have money in my life! Having it would mean betraying my values and my understanding of integrity. As soon as I realized that, other things began to make sense. It was no wonder I never had any money, and that when I did I would get rid of it as soon as possible by spending it or giving it away, and even by accumulating massive debt. Keeping myself at a safe distance from money meant angry creditors, stacks of unopened bills, and chronic chaos. And all this had happened unconsciously; my money beliefs were running my life without my even knowing what was happening or why.

I am certain that it was not my parents' intention to teach me about money this way, or to convey the message that money means conflict. But that's what happens when we learn indirectly; we acquire our lessons haphazardly.

It's important to realize that not all money learning is negative and to acknowledge the money learning that has served us well. Fortunately, I gleaned other money lessons from my parents that were beneficial. For example, if there was a sin in my father's house, it was doing work you didn't love, which he believed was morally wrong. Furthermore, my dad lived by this: He pursued work that he loved and made good money doing it. He didn't model a healthy relationship in other ways, but he taught—and proved—that work could be aligned with happiness.

This was powerful modeling. I didn't realize until much later in life that this stance was a unique and special gift. As a result, I have spent my life doing what I love. I can honestly say that with a few brief exceptions, I have always enjoyed my work and felt compelled to pursue my dreams, whether they made sense to others or not. I've always had the freedom to choose career paths based solely on whether they inspired and excited me. Since my work is directly related to the flow of money in my life, this is a money belief that is in full alignment with my values. Consequently, money has almost always come to me by doing work I love.

It is important to note that though I've benefited from this belief about work throughout my life, only when I changed my relationship with money was I able to reap the financial benefits of my work without unconsciously undermining myself. Until then, when money came to me, my other money beliefs would sabotage how I handled it. I had to do my own Spiritual Finance work to realize that to have a healthy relationship with money, I would have to change all beliefs that were not in alignment with my values. I would have to understand what was driving my behavior and change what wasn't working. Once I did this, I experienced personal and professional financial freedom. I also began to realize that the lessons I had absorbed from my environment had been running my life, always lurking just beneath the surface of my awareness.

In neither of the money learning instances I've

shared, one negative and one positive, did my father know he was teaching me about money; we rarely even spoke about money. But those two shaped my life. Consider, for instance, my belief that money equals conflict. This was clearly out of alignment with my core values—but how could I change it? I decided that a belief that would work for me would be that money equals *connection*. I do not value conflict, but I do value connection; by shifting the belief, I could be in alignment with both my values and money. This new belief, that money creates connection, has allowed me to give money a place in my life.

Discovering where our money beliefs come from can be fascinating. Once we understand their origins, we can make sense of why money shows up the way it does in our lives. Though our money learning may have occurred haphazardly, the results are not. Our beliefs run the show, even if we aren't aware of what they are or where they came from. The good news is that we can change them.

It's Personal

My brother's relationship with money is different from mine. Though we're only two years apart and grew up within the same family dynamic, he learned a separate set of money lessons. This is evidenced by how dramatically our money relationships have diverged. One example is the exchange between my parents that taught me that money equals conflict; that was a lesson he didn't receive.

Maybe it was just because he was out the door first that day; maybe it was because I'm the elder. I will never know and it doesn't matter. What does matter is that we can't decipher our own relationship with money by observing anyone else's. Even though my brother and I were in basically the same place at the same time, I learned a debilitating money lesson. He did not. Each relationship is different and, ultimately, a unique and authentic expression of the person's lifetime of experiences with money.

Most Fascinating Research Project

Your money relationship is yours to figure out; no one else can do it for you. I encourage you to make yourself your most fascinating research project.

Learning about money doesn't stop with childhood. You may have even learned something about money yesterday or today. When you're aware of what you're learning, you can call it into question. But this is a choice. If you don't know that you're learning something, you may take it in unconsciously—yet it can influence your thoughts, behavior, and actions in powerful ways.

By making yourself your most fascinating research project, you can discover not only your money beliefs, but where they came from. You can decide whether they fit you, and if not, custom tailor beliefs that are in perfect alignment with your values.

Cultivating awareness is a crucial element in changing your relationship with money. Once you know something you can never return to not knowing it. By actively cultivating awareness of your relationship with money—by understanding where you are now and gaining clarity about how you got here—you will be able to move forward.

In the exchange between my parents that I described, I could have learned many things. That money equals anxiety, anger, separation, pain, suffering … the list is long and for me, the lesson was that money equals conflict. Yet that belief doesn't fit with my spiritual values; if I allowed that belief to exist, I could not have a healthy relationship with money. So I decided to change it: I don't value conflict. I do value connection. Money, therefore, began to equal connection.

Since deciding to change that belief, I have seen the truth of it all around me. Every person I encounter has something in common with me: We all have a relationship with money—the person who just passed me on the highway, the clerk in the grocery store, the actor on television, my son. We are all connected this way.

Furthermore, when I ask people in my Spiritual Finance classes to talk about money, I notice how, even though it may seem foreign and feel awkward at first, once they begin to open up, they connect with one another quickly. Despite their sometimes dramatic cultural, societal, religious, political, generational, or economic differences, how they feel about and relate to money is often quite similar. They discover that they have more in common than they ever would have imagined. They are connected. Money equals connection.

Our beliefs create the lens through which we perceive the world and others in it. When we adjust our vision, we can adjust how the world looks. When we change our beliefs about money so that they are in alignment with our values, the way money shows up in our lives and how we interact with it will begin to change, and often dramatically.

As you unravel the mystery of your money beliefs, you will gain clarity, begin to make choices, and become empowered in this important relationship. By noticing and reinforcing positive learning, you can use your beliefs more mindfully and effectively to build confidence in your relationship with money and interact with it in a new and liberating way.

Taboo

I grew up believing that it wasn't polite to talk about money—which further implied that people who did talk openly about it (who were usually wealthy) were vulgar. Therefore, since we never talked about it and no one I knew (who wasn't vulgar) ever talked about it, everything related to money felt secret and mysterious. No wonder I didn't understand it! This belief, or some version of it, is quite common. It always shows up in our initial survey about money in the Spiritual Finance class. Words that describe this belief, and its implications, have included secret, private, nobody else's business, hidden, mysterious, and even shameful; no wonder money is kept in the closet.

We guard the details of our relationship with money with great care, because it reflects our self-worth, our judgments about ourselves, and how we believe others perceive us. It can be scary territory, loaded with our limiting, and frequently fearful, beliefs about money. It takes courage to challenge this societal norm and speak openly on such an intimate topic. What will happen if people know who we really are in relation to money?

You're Not Alone

The biggest secret was revealed when I began talking candidly about money. I was surprised to learn that I wasn't the only one who felt as I did, and I certainly wasn't the only one who had learned about money haphazardly. I found out that my experience was quite common, shared perhaps by a majority of people. Furthermore, despite some initial awkwardness, talking openly about money wasn't even difficult. Most people are surprised by how quickly they become comfortable talking about money; this is often an eye-opening moment for people who engage in this exploration. The moment we begin having conversations about money, we realize that others are just as challenged in their relationships with money as we are. This was a huge awakening for me.

Suddenly, I wasn't alone—on my tiny, deserted island with no other land in sight. The truth is that we are surrounded by people in similar circumstances, with similarly limiting beliefs. Once we start sharing our stories, we realize that we're one among many.

Once I understood that I wasn't alone, I was

less hard on myself. For instance, I learned that I could look around for some way-finding assistance. People who had already navigated beyond where I was helped me chart a course to a more prosperous land, one that I am now happy to call home. We are not alone on this journey.

It's Not the Amount

In our culture, there's an assumption that suffering—or the lack thereof—in relationship with money must be linked to the amount of money you have. The more money you have, the easier, freer, and less stressful your life and your relationship with money will be.

Not necessarily. In my own relationship with money, when I sometimes had very little, and other times earned large amounts, there were underlying patterns. Regardless of the amount of money I had, for instance, I was always anxious and stressed. Inevitably, I'd get rid of money in ways that created chaos. I did this unconsciously. Sometimes there was much more to get rid of than at other times, but my bad relationship with money ran my life regardless of how much money I had, and it was never enough.

It doesn't seem to matter how much money people have; I've heard, in essence, the same story from people in radically different economic situations. It's not how much money we have, but rather our relationship with it that determines whether we suffer or thrive.

In the initial survey in the Spiritual Finance class, in which I ask people to describe money, I often hear the word "shame." It has been spoken by people in poverty and by millionaires. I've come to realize that shame is an equal-opportunity emotion, one that's felt by people who don't have enough to meet their basic needs and — surprising to me at first — by people who have much more than they need.

Certainly, types of suffering can vary widely. Yet if we are in a bad relationship with money — to a lot of money, not enough money, or anywhere in between — it can feel the same. And it will have similar debilitating effects on our quality of life, our relationships, and our health. Fortunately, I have learned that this kind of suffering is optional.

Part II — Getting Real

Getting Real

Most of us aren't even aware of our relationship with money. The relationship is barely present, and we are doing as little as possible to get by. If any other relationship were described this way, trouble—if it wasn't there already—would likely be on its way.

Every spiritual practice involves getting real: creating an intimate understanding of what is present. By exploring the reality you've created with money, you'll be able to begin finding out where you are now.

You've been learning about money through-out your entire life—picking up lessons here and there over the course of many years. These lessons have been integrated into how you think about money, work, other people, and society, and often in ways you weren't aware of. Yet these subtle lessons have affected the way you act, react to, and interact with everything related to money, and it will probably take a while to effectively change.

If you don't know where you are, how you got here, or where you're going, your navigation skills will be faulty at best and, at worst, nonexistent. It's not fun to be wandering in the money wilderness, unable to discern which map will guide you to better territory. Successful navigation requires the answers to two questions: "Where am I now?" and "What is my destination?" In the process of changing your core relationship with money, it is also helpful to know how you got here in the first place. This awareness will create a more empowered perspective: the perspective of choice.

This means opening your eyes and getting acquainted with anything you've been avoiding. This is a necessary first step, and though it may seem daunting, almost certainly it won't be as painful as you imagine. This was a difficult step for me to take. Because my financial situation was dire, I didn't want to acknowledge the reality of my situation; I believed that if I did, my worst fears would be realized. So I avoided the details—yet those details added up to the big picture. It was like viewing a mural through a drinking straw. It was time to throw away the straw, open my eyes, and get real.

Breaking Down

Huddled in a corner, making myself as tiny as possible. Wrenching emotions and crying so hard that it felt like my insides were coming out. The terror I'd shoved down was finally exploding up and out. I hadn't lost my closest friend or found out that I was dying; I had just gotten off the phone with a creditor.

That specific call wasn't remarkable, since it was one of hundreds such calls that I'd received. What set this one apart was that it was my own personal breaking point. Though this happened many years ago, the memory still leaves me raw. On the surface, it seems ridiculous: Why would I fall apart simply because someone had asked me for money? Yet I was terrified—afraid I would lose my home, my business, and my livelihood. I was afraid I would be homeless, and that I wouldn't be able to feed or clothe myself or my young son; somehow, I would lose him as well.

I was so paralyzed by fear, I didn't know how much I owed or to whom. I didn't know whether my creditors could actually take things away from me, but they kept saying they could. And, in the grip of my terror, I believed them.

I had piles of unopened mail—bills and late notices, threats and reality—I hadn't looked at, because if I did I might find out that things were even worse than I imagined. I avoided the mail, the phone, and the entire mess I had created until I couldn't deny it any longer. And finally, at that moment of breaking down, I stopped trying to hide.

It was the painful beginning of a long, and deeply personal, process. Though it felt like everything was ending, in truth it was my first step. Backed into a corner, I opened my eyes to the chaos I had created and knew that I had to change my relationship with money.

At that time I would have described the relationship as adversarial at best. I didn't like money, I didn't trust money, I considered it unreliable, and there was no place for it in my life. I had banished money. And now, like it or not, I needed it back. If I wanted the situation to change, I had no choice.

When you have to remain in a relationship that's adversarial, what do you do? You start somewhere. It may take a long time to repair—and forgive the damage that's been done—but you start somewhere. So that's what I did.

A Relationship With Money

Imagine that money is a person: a walking, talking, thinking, breathing, eating, drinking, going-to-the-movies-on-a-Friday-night person. Imagine this person materializing in front of you. What is your first impression? How do you feel? Do you like them, or not? Have you spoken recently, or is there a lack of communication, maybe even the silent treatment? Have you been avoiding them, or have they been avoiding you? Do you trust them? Do you respect and have faith in them, or is your relationship quite different?

When people describe great relationships, they typically use descriptors such as open, friendly, communicative, loving, caring, compassionate, trusting, safe, warm, happy, comforting, and fulfilling. Consider a fulfilling relationship that you have, or once had, in your life. How would you describe it? Compare this description to how you'd describe your relationship with money. Are there differences? There usually are.

Our relationship with money can include deep and meaningful spiritual lessons, if we are receptive to them. If your description of a fulfilling relationship with another person differs from how you describe your relationship with money, it's time to change it—to bring it into alignment with how you'd describe any other positive relationship.

When I propose viewing money as a person, people have an immediate response. A vision emerges in which they imagine "money" walking through the door. That first impression reveals a lot about how you perceive, and relate to, money.

The gender we assign to "money" can be intriguing. I ask people for their first impressions, and get varied responses: a man in a suit, a menacing dark cloud, a dollar bill with arms, legs, and a masculine face—but rarely a female presence. I've introduced hundreds of people to this way of thinking about money, and I can count, on my two hands, the number of times money has been perceived, from the first, as feminine. This is interesting and, particularly from a cultural perspective, revealing.

Consider what your first impression reveals about how you think about money, what you believe about money, and how you relate to money. What if you were to change your image of money? How would you change it, and how would that affect your relationship? What if you thought of money as a benevolent presence whose values are completely in alignment with your own? Would a different image of money affect how you relate to and behave around it?

I encourage people to experiment with this image of money as a person, trying out different identities for money to see how each one fits. Personalities have many facets. Imagine that you can explore money's personality and shape it into a multifaceted, supportive presence just for you—perhaps in a way that would enable you to perceive money as a friend. What qualities do you value most in a friend or trusted advisor? Give them to money and see how it feels.

What does a healthy relationship require? Becoming authentic and healing the rifts that have been created by your history. Integrating your money consciousness with your whole being, including your values. Creating awareness of—and a belief system about—money that empowers and supports you. When you engage in this exploration, your relationship to money and finance—to abundance and prosperity—will deepen and thrive.

Uniquely Human

A dog possesses a unique dog-ness. A bird, a fern, a stone: All have distinct and immutable characteristics. As humans, we don't have a hand in choosing such traits, but we do with money. Money can't exist without us. We create it; we determine its value and qualities; we decide how we will use it and think about it. We create the relationship we have, and this makes money uniquely human.

Because we create it, we have the power to change it. This is exciting, because we can reimagine it anytime we want. Using the same tools we use to change how we relate to other people, we can change our relationship with money. Just like human relationships, our relationship with money thrives on presence, attention, and engagement.

Eyes Wide Open

I was afraid to look at the piles of unopened mail. So my first step was to open my eyes, screw up my courage, face what I had created, and get to know it. I had to be bigger than my fear and pick up a letter opener.

I opened the mail one envelope at a time. Confronting my money reality, I sorted through a pile until I couldn't take it any longer. When I started hyperventilating, I'd stop. I'd scream, or take a walk around my little house, or sit with my head between my knees until the panic subsided. Then I would pick up the letter opener again. It was a process. I was frightened, but I made it through. After years of avoiding this task, I opened my mail and opened my eyes. It was bad, but not as bad as I thought it would be—and I learned something quite freeing:

The unknown is always scarier than the known.

I learned that when I know what I'm dealing with, I am in a position of choice and empowerment. By opening my bills, I faced my reality. I could then take action and begin making changes. At that point, I was finally able to take a deep breath.

Although it didn't feel like it at first, I had options and I could look for solutions. When I was still in the unknown, however, none of that was available to me. I was lost on the fringes of nowhere with no map or compass. No options available, no solution in sight. Now, given a choice, I've learned to opt for awareness and information.

A Great Place to Grow From

At times, as you create your new relationship with money, your reality will shift. Sometimes this is the result of a slow and gradual process, during which you shift gracefully into this new way of being; sometimes awareness arrives abruptly, like blinders being ripped off. What was once dark and unknown is flooded with the blinding light of truth, and that can be hard at first to endure. The reality you thought you were living is suddenly altered, and it can take time to adjust to this new awareness. To encourage people during this process, I share this with them:

> *When it looks like shit, smells like shit, and feels like shit, that just means that it's really great fertilizer. It's a great place to grow from.*

In my first career, working with Thoroughbred racehorses, I spent a lot of time on farms and with farmers. I was taught to appreciate manure, which is regarded as more precious than gold. In other words, the stinkiest thing on the farm is one of the most valuable: It may not look or smell good to begin with, but what it can do for the farmer is not just valuable, it's essential.

Just like my appreciation for manure's potential, I respect those moments in life that are the toughest, when we are challenged to grow. Like manure, the situations that are the most difficult can also be the most valuable. Where you are now with money may look and feel stinky, but this is fertile soil for growth.

Be Like a Sea Sponge

Sea sponges don't do a whole lot; they are sustained by the circulation of water around and through them. The action of their environment provides nutrition and removes waste. When you create a deliberate change in your perceptions of money, it's as if you've switched your water supply to one that's purer. It will help you grow, and remove unhealthy beliefs and behavior. This, in itself, is a fundamental change.

Do not underestimate the power of awareness. It is the single most critical step in any change process, and it may be all you need to begin to improve your relationship with money. Once you've achieved awareness, there is no going back to that place of ignorance. Don't expect your life to be the same as it was before; the process can be unsettling.

When a big shift has occurred, we may get an urge to do something with it, quick! Before it goes away. But in all the clamor, we can create even more chaos. Instead, trust that your new awareness, coupled with taking simple steps to get real, is changing your life significantly—even though it may feel as if things aren't moving fast enough.

You don't have to do anything drastic. Absorb your new awareness like a sea sponge in the ocean: Just rock, gently, back and forth, letting the change flow over and through you, into the core of you. Absorb it—just like a sea sponge. By integrating your new awareness, you're already taking the biggest step forward on your Spiritual Finance journey.

Challenge Your Assumptions

The IRS is mean, right? I assumed it was, based on cultural stereotypes—until I picked up the phone and called them, in response to a number of unopened certified letters, and found out that I was wrong. They didn't burn me at the stake; in fact, the representative spoke to me like a real person, not a faceless number. I was told, clearly and succinctly, what my options were, and the shaky ground I was standing on became a little bit firmer. I discovered that the IRS is great at telling us about the ground beneath our feet. I also found out that they only wanted the money I owed them, and that they would work with me to help that happen. They were even kind, and it was one of the best customer service experiences I've ever had. My assumptions were completely wrong.

It wasn't sweet and syrupy, mind you, and I'm sure this isn't how it always works. There were a lot of hard, cold facts that I didn't know how to deal with. I had an IRS tax debt that would choke an elephant, which I had created out of a series of uninformed and in-denial mistakes. As I began to move forward, I learned that I needed to challenge all of my assumptions—not just the ones about the IRS.

I had to challenge my assumption that if I called the electric company they would terminate my electricity even sooner than the shutoff date, or refuse to accept anything less than the entire balance. I also challenged my assumption that nothing could be done about my mortgage, which was in default, and that the credit card companies would show up with a moving van, fill it with everything I owned, and take it away if I didn't do exactly what they wanted.

My assumptions were based on fear, and fear is rarely rational. I'm a creative person, and if I imagine a worst-case scenario, it will be exponentially more cataclysmic than the actual worst-case scenario. When I challenge my blown-out-of-proportion assumptions, however, I find out that I'm not going to spontaneously combust. Things are almost always better than I've imagined, there are options available, and I've wasted time and energy working myself into a frenzy. When I challenge my assumptions I reach sound conclusions faster, with less pain, and I am often pleasantly surprised by the results.

Personal Responsibility

Once I had confronted reality, taken a few deep breaths, started some conversations, asked for some help, and taken the first steps on my Spiritual Finance journey, I realized that this was a mess I had created all by myself. Nobody else had done this to me — not the big bad creditors, my parents, my ex-husband, or my ex-employer. I was responsible for all of it.

This was difficult to admit. But when I finally stopped blaming other people for my predicament, I realized that if I could do it, I could undo it. If I had singlehandedly, and creatively, caused this financial worst-case scenario, I could now choose to create my best-case scenario.

A Process

You've been accumulating money beliefs throughout your entire life. From the time you began comprehending language and paying attention to people's behavior, these beliefs have affected how you've behaved with money and created the relationship you have now. How old are you? The number of years you've been alive is close to the number of years you've been learning about money, probably without even knowing it. This type of learning doesn't change overnight; it's a process.

Changing our relationship with money is like bringing light into a dark room. We tend to assume that once we view the world from a new perspective, a switch has been flipped, and everything is instantly different. This is rarely the case, however; it's more like a dimmer switch.

Change is gradual. It gets brighter in increments that may not seem to be changing anything, but over time these increments of brightness add up to clarity and insight. With attention and consistency, and by cultivating an awareness that creates new beliefs and behaviors, our relationship with money becomes steadily brighter.

Part III — Moving Forward

Moving Forward

Now it's time to move forward with some new tools and perspectives, toward specific destinations clearly aligned with your values. By developing more awareness, taking action to change patterns and behaviors, and cultivating mastery, you will steadily progress — with money as a powerful ally on your journey.

Your previous experience with money is in the past. You can behave differently from now on, make better choices, and deliberately choose your money beliefs by examining the beliefs you've accumulated and deciding what fits and what doesn't, what stays and what goes. Though the process may be gradual, everything about your relationship with money can change.

Start the Conversation

While still in the throes of my financial recovery, I had a goal to attend an intensive leadership program that had a hefty price tag. Because of my financial situation, I assumed this goal was unattainable. Hearing my longing, my coach offered a brilliant but simple suggestion: "Just start the conversation." I thought, Have the conversation, even though I was sure I could never make it happen? It seemed ridiculous—but what did I have to lose? The worst-case scenario was that I'd confirm my assumptions and stay exactly where I already was. The best-case scenario was that I would learn something new, and there would be a way to realize my dream sooner than I imagined.

I called the training company, attended a phone informational session, and learned there were options that my assumptions had discounted. I was still convinced it was impossible, but at least I was engaged in the conversation. And the more it progressed, the more information and confidence I gained — enough that I began submitting paperwork, received a partial scholarship, secured reasonable financing, and booked my flight to begin the program in just over a month. A few weeks earlier I had been certain it was impossible, and suddenly it was happening. It was challenging for me to confront my assumptions, but by starting the conversation, I found out that those assumptions were incorrect.

Thanks to what I learned in that leadership program, I've developed in ways I never expected. I'm now comfortable presenting to large groups — in fact, I thrive there — which has expanded my business and paid off exponentially, both professionally and personally, in myriad ways. Starting one conversation changed my life. Conversations can also shift things in smaller ways that eventually add up to big changes.

Assumptions inform our actions, and though sometimes correct, they are more often guided by fear. They tell us what things cost, what the options are, what's possible, and what isn't. We assume all sorts of things, and it's easy to get stuck in the underlying fears and limiting beliefs our assumptions represent. Sometimes it's blatant, like my thoughts about the IRS, and other times it's more subtle, like discounting possibilities before I've even explored them. Regardless of the scope, our assumptions keep us from moving forward. Move toward your goals by challenging your assumptions, starting the conversation, asking questions, and examining the facts. You might be pleasantly surprised.

Worth

Changing my relationship with money was a quest. Obsessed with cracking the code of my mysterious relationship with money, I learned as much as possible. One of the most enlightening tools I discovered along the way was the net worth calculation. Net worth is simply your total liabilities subtracted from your total assets, revealing your financial bottom line.

I had barely embraced opening an envelope, never mind approaching money in ways that required a calculator and would yield a reality check. This calculation would expose my financial reality, and I was scared that it would be negative. This fear epitomized the misguided way I felt about myself—that I had no value. I had never looked at the total picture, and it was time to face up to it.

I began plugging in numbers, and when I didn't have a figure, I'd search tirelessly until I found it. Finally, with all the numbers in front of me, I calculated my bottom line. Tapping away at the calculator, my net worth revealed itself. In disbelief, I punched the numbers in repeatedly, and every time, the calculation revealed the same thing—I had a positive net worth! I was shocked. Even though my situation was desperate, I felt like I had value, when I had previously assumed I had none. I knew, intellectually, that money doesn't determine the value of a person, but that was exactly what I had done to myself.

I'd perceived myself as having debt worth, not net worth, operating from the perspective of my financial value equaling debt, but this was just one part of the picture. The other part was the value of my assets, and I had never considered adding that to the equation. Now that I had, it turned my world around. Instead of thinking of myself from the perspective of debt worth, I could see my relationship with money more clearly.

This simple calculation changed the way I felt about myself, and since that day, I've tracked my net worth. It provides a quick snapshot of my financial health, and as with anything else, the more you pay attention to it, the healthier the relationship will be. In the first six months my net worth doubled, and since then it has become consistently more positive. I take action to help that happen, and by keeping an eye on it, I stay engaged and can appreciate my results. It's a useful and motivating tool.

It's not uncommon to have a perspective of debt worth. The ones who regard themselves from its opposite, the perspective of net worth, were taught—directly or through modeling—to have an awareness of their assets, not just their debt. Growing up, I recall many times when I was aware of debt, but few times when the value of family assets was discussed, and it provided a skewed, incomplete picture. The net worth calculation helped me fill in the missing pieces, shifting my view.

Suggesting the net worth calculation often brings groans, or even shortness of breath, to my

Spiritual Finance class participants, but it is consistently one of the most helpful tools. Calculating net worth provides a more accurate, complete, and informed picture of where we are now.

Conscious Spending

Our spending is often habitual, programmed, or reactionary. Frequently, there's money in a checking account or wallet, and the next thing we know, the money is gone. But where did it go? Daily transactions can add up quickly without our remaining aware of what's happening or the consequences. This creates money patterns that are rooted in impulse or emotions and make it difficult to meet financial obligations.

When spending patterns are unconscious, chaos inevitably results. Decisions are motivated by our underlying beliefs about money, which may or may not be aligned with our values; how can we know whether they are, if we're not aware of what we're doing? Examining our spending provides clues about our values. The things that we feel good about spending money on are likely to be in alignment with our values. The things we avoid spending on are likely to be out of alignment with our values, or reflect a belief about money.

One example is how comfortable I feel buying hay and grain: A well-stocked supply of quality hay and grain is aligned with my values and makes me feel wealthy. My animals are important, and I feel grounded and happy caring for them. Happiness, groundedness, and agriculture are all things I value. I also purchase my supplies from a business run by a family I respect, whose products are fairly priced and of good quality. The sellers are reliable, kind, generous, and their business adds value to the community. As an example of their generosity, one day they noticed that one of my tires looked a little flat. Though I probably would have been fine driving home, they insisted on putting air in the tire for me—exemplifying my own values of kindness, generosity, and service.

I found another spending clue, which took a long time to decipher, at the gas station. I consistently avoided purchasing gasoline, often waiting until the fuel gauge was in the red empty zone. (My fiancé would confirm this. Nearly every time he got into my car, the gas gauge was on empty. If he was going to drive my car, he'd have to take it to the gas station before he did anything else.) For years I tried to figure it out, but my avoidance stymied me. When I had plenty of money I'd avoid it; whether gas prices were up or down, it didn't matter. Environmental concerns weren't the answer, either. I work from home, and unless I have to go somewhere, I generally stay put; my yearly mileage is ridiculously low. Yet even though I'd been working on my relationship with money for years, I couldn't figure out how the gas station was out of alignment with my values.

One day my fuel gauge was perched on empty, and I groaned as I reluctantly pulled up to the pump. I filled the tank, got back in the car, and smelled gasoline on my hands. Yuck! This was the reason I never wanted to purchase gas! I can't stand the smell of it, and I value beautiful aromas. Finally, I'd solved the mystery. It was a little thing that had big consequences.

I don't like the smell of gasoline, so I avoided spending money on it. This had put me in jeopardy of running out of gas on the side of the road countless times, but since I didn't understand why I was doing it, I wasn't empowered to change. Since I've become aware of what motivated my behavior, I've changed this pattern by reframing it. I now think about how buying gas is in alignment with my values. I value freedom, timeliness, and safety, and by keeping the gas tank filled, I can just get in and go whenever I want (freedom), I don't have to stop when I'm en route to a scheduled meeting (timeliness), and I don't have to worry about running out of gas on the side of the road (safety). Collectively, these values outweigh the minor inconvenience of smelling gasoline—and I can always wash my hands. This small thing dictated my behavior for decades.

We all have our own unique spending patterns. We spend money on some things comfortably and we avoid others. Patterns that are out of alignment with our values will unconsciously create suffering and chaos—but by creating the habit of making decisions informed by our values, spending feels different. By making conscious spending decisions, we understand how we are honoring our values, how they are helping us navigate toward our goals, and how this will affect our relationship with money: It will feel peaceful and empowering.

Presence

How we organize our finances reveals how present we are in relationship with money. The phrase "As without, so within" implies that our external environment is aligned with our internal environment. I ask people to test this perspective by looking in their wallet to see what it reveals.

The first time I did this, my wallet was a mess—disorganized and chaotic, and I had no idea how much money there was—a clear portrayal of my inner money landscape. Today, I usually know what's in my wallet, and it's well organized—which demonstrates how much my relationship with money has changed. The same theme applies to other ways I organized money and finances. When I first began changing my relationship with money, my organizational system wasn't a system at all. Stacks of unopened envelopes and paperwork crammed into disorderly files reflected how I related to money: I didn't. If I needed to find something it took a long time, and I avoided looking.

Though organizing my wallet was an easy first step, finding a system for organizing the rest of my finances took longer, and continues to evolve. I tried everything—dated organizers, calendar alerts on my computer, and many other things that weren't a good fit. Those things undoubtedly work for some people, but not for me. Sometimes I'd get stuck in the rut of a not-working method. But then I'd try something else, until I discovered what worked; nobody could tell me what was best for me.

Spreadsheets are a good fit for some people, but others feel more comfortable with pencil and paper. A filing cabinet might work well for one person, while another feels more connected to money using handcrafted folders. However you organize your finances, choose a method that's custom tailored to reflect *your* personality and values.

If you're artistic, for instance, like bright colors, and love to journal, you'll be well served by a system with those attributes. If you like a linear, straightforward approach, look for techniques with those qualities. You should feel comfortable enough with the way you organize your finances that the process doesn't discourage you from being present. Your system should feel inviting—something you're inspired to spend time with. Experiment until you find the system that encourages you to stay present with money.

What Do You Want?

There is no standard, one-size-fits-all relationship with money. We've each arrived at this point in life through a series of individual experiences, and as we continue to evolve, our values are our own to define and redefine. To enjoy a fulfilling and supportive relationship with money, the relationship must be customized to who we are—informed by where we've been and where we're going—and you are the only person who can define this for yourself.

What do you want? That question can stop people in their tracks. As strange as it seems, we're often unaware that we can, and should, ask ourselves this question. But without this exploration, we're vulnerable to an unfulfilling and bland life experience that, potentially, can lead to unhappiness, despair, and resentment. Thankfully, the answer to this essential question can eliminate that possibility. What do *you* want?

Wealth

Call it wealth, abundance, prosperity; it's all the same thing—and it's different for everybody. What does wealth mean to you? Though our society perpetuates a stereotypical portrayal of wealth, wealth can take as many forms as there are people. It's helpful to get acquainted with your particular view. I've discussed wealth with many people; some aspire to a vision similar to the one portrayed by the media, while others aim for a life of simplicity and modest sufficiency. The range of interpretation is enormous. I like to begin the exploration with the inquiry: "What feels wealthy to you?"

For myself, when I imagine how wealth feels, several things immediately come to mind, such as a barn stocked with feed and hay. I feel abundant and prosperous when I walk into the feed room, breathe the aroma of hay, lift the feed-bin lid, and scoop into a generous supply of grain. Other aspects of wealth include having plenty of time to do what I want, being engaged with work I love, having the freedom to set my own schedule, and being completely debt free. These images and desires provide valuable navigational assistance as I progress in my relationship with money. Each person's vision will be unique.

One man I know, who has a fabulous relationship with money, has a very different wealth picture. While I aim to have no debt in my life, he hopes to accumulate a lot of debt, and specifically, mortgages. For him, wealth means having a lot of assets, which he intends to acquire by amassing debt; to him, this feels empowering. When I try this picture on for size, it doesn't fit; it feels burdensome and stressful. In other words, one person's empowerment can be another's encumbrance.

Cultivate curiosity about your definition by identifying your most important values, then let them inform your ideas about wealth, prosperity, and abundance. What would feel most fulfilling? Use this self-inquiry to inform your money choices, so that you can consistently navigate toward your view of wealth.

A Moral Imperative

When we think about money, other things are implied, such as wealth and work. In my father's view, there was a moral imperative inherent to money, which he clearly communicated. I was raised with the understanding that doing work I didn't love was wrong. I was expected to pursue work I loved, and that was something I wouldn't dare challenge. I am fiercely loyal to this perspective, and it has served me well.

I believe we're meant to express the best of ourselves to provide service to the world, and if we don't love our work, we can't channel our truest selves. It's a misuse of time, energy, talents, and our intrinsic gifts. Furthermore, if we do work that we dislike, we are doing someone else's job—and they need to be there, so that people can benefit from their joyous presence.

Sometimes, we can see a job as a means to an end, moving us to another place in life, but I see too much temptation in that perspective for my own comfort. I believe in both: That we can have a job that supports us along the way to our ultimate goals, while simultaneously providing joy and happiness. When we're audacious enough to believe this, it's amazing how often it happens. Even my most menial jobs (and I've had many) have been fun and enlivening while providing the sustenance for me to move forward along my path.

This perspective is in alignment with my values. It may not fully honor yours, but I've found that when people explore what they want in life, most embrace this belief. Since most people's modeling regarding work and career has differed from mine, it can seem like an improbable shift. But what if we considered it a moral imperative for our work to be fully aligned with our values, every step of the way?

Life is short. What do you love? Gather clues, and whenever there's an opportunity to move in the direction of joy-filled work, take a small step. Start the conversation, do the research, and get curious. As long as you believe you can, it will be possible to have a healthy relationship with money while enjoying fulfilling, rewarding work.

The Flow of Money

Sometimes I hold onto money because I fear not having enough. Clutching too tightly, however, slows the flow of resources. When I've delayed paying bills, and examine my behavior closely, I can usually identify the fear. When I release my grip, the flow of money inevitably increases.

Other times, I get rid of money too quickly. When I'm circulating it away from myself like a raging river, it reveals how uncomfortable I am with receiving and being provided for — how unworthy or shameful I feel. When it's gushing through my life, it doesn't have time to nourish and sustain me, and this usually indicates that I'm making undermining financial choices. Only by confronting my fears can I resolve them and allow myself to experience the flow of money and the abundance it brings.

By becoming aware of how money flows into and out of our lives, we can determine what a healthy flow feels like; once we've identified it, we can use it as something to aim for. When grasping too tightly, let go a bit. When getting rid of money too quickly, slow the pace.

The tendencies and habits we have regarding the flow of money can feel awkward to challenge at first. But when we behave differently, we confront the limiting beliefs that informed the behavior in the first place, providing a perfect opportunity to cultivate awareness and change our beliefs and behavior.

Give Money a Purpose

When people tell me they want more money, my first question is "Why?" Not because I think more money is a bad thing, but because I'm intrigued: What is money's purpose, and how can it be aligned with our values? Sometimes we think we want more money just because we *should* want more. This feels like a cultural assumption. Thinking about the purpose for money invites a deeper exploration.

When we give money a direction aligned with our values, it tends to move toward that destination with more flow. This response isn't coming from money; it's coming from us. When we're clear about how money is supporting our values, and our purpose in the world, we can clear the limiting beliefs, patterns, and habits that have blocked us from creating and receiving it in the past. When money is not consciously aligned with our values, we are more likely to undermine our financial results.

When aiming for something that will provide financial gain, carefully consider its purpose. Where will the money flow? How will it support your values? Be specific, making sure that the purpose is aligned with your values and reflects your view of wealth, abundance, and prosperity. The more deliberately you do this, the more you will positively affect the flow of money. Just like any other relationship, your relationship with money will thrive when it has mindful purpose.

Receive

Without a receiver, we cannot give. By gracefully receiving, we give the gift of giving back to the giver, and it's one of the most generous things we can offer. It feels great to give, but feels unfulfilling when the gifts we offer are not received. By not receiving, we rob the giver of their full experience of giving.

In Spiritual Finance, I assign homework on becoming a masterful receiver in all areas of our lives—not just with money—and I offer some guidelines for masterful receiving.

When you're given something — a gift, a compliment, money, anything — say "Thank you," and nothing else. When we're uncomfortable with receiving, there's a tendency to dismiss or diminish the gift by immediately giving something back, or implying that the giver "shouldn't have." When we're the giver, this response can be hurtful; it's one of the reasons we love giving to children so much. Before children have been taught—intentionally or not—that receiving is somehow bad, or that giving is preferable, they are usually great receivers. They overflow with gratitude, and it feels wonderful for the giver, since they, in turn, receive a full experience of giving.

When you're receiving, remain open in your physical posture. Turning away, crossing your arms, slouching, or avoiding eye contact will block receipt of the gift. Stay open.

Keep breathing! Holding our breath is another

way of blocking the experience of receiving. Remaining physically open and present with the giver, while taking a full, deep breath offers a unique opportunity for the giver to experience giving, and for us to fully experience receiving.

Be sure not to "grab and go." This is a way of physically avoiding the experience of receiving. When we walk away before we fully experience receiving the gift, we are also walking away with the giver's experience of giving.

Resist the urge to have a "tennis match." This happens most frequently with compliments. One person gives a compliment, and the receiver immediately lobs another back in return. It can go back and forth without either person experiencing the gift. Stop! Receive! You can always give something back later if you want to, but for the moment, practice receiving the gift that's been given.

If we've avoided receiving in the past, these receiving practices can make us feel vulnerable and awkward at first. Being a graceful receiver can take practice, but will eventually get easier. This was certainly my experience, since I used to be one of the world's worst receivers. It wasn't until I was forced to receive help, in order to change my relationship with money, that I began learning how to receive.

It wasn't easy. I'd been a serial giver, not allowing anyone to help or give to me, and it got me into a lot of trouble, financially and personally. As I began practicing the art of receiving, I had to face the feelings of shame and unworthiness I'd been avoiding. That made me squirm at first, and it took courage to persevere—but now I'm a masterful receiver, and it feels wonderful. Learning to receive has opened up a flow of money that is more fulfilling and allows me to give more freely. As I receive more, I am able to give more.

Create a New Cycle

It's one thing to have an intellectual understanding and quite another to put it into practice—and something else entirely to make it stick. By changing our awareness about money, we change our minds, but that's only part of the process. The other part is to put that awareness into action in ways that create a new cycle. Action, discipline, and continued attention are required to sustain the change and avoid returning to old patterns and habits. This is a real turning point, and doesn't happen overnight. The habits we're unlearning were developed over a lifetime, and can be particularly sticky. It takes willingness to endure the awkwardness of learning something new to create sustained change.

Many times I've witnessed the repetition of lifelong cycles. People shift their awareness and take action to improve their relationship with money, but fail to weave in the support, accountability, and discipline needed to sustain those changes long enough to create a new cycle. They think they're done when they've barely begun. This is the danger of financial advice that tells us what to do, but doesn't combine it with awareness about our relationship with money. We need to understand where our behavior comes from to change it effectively. Without this type of awareness, followed by continued discipline and support, self-sabotage and repetitive cycles are commonplace.

I've experienced this personally. In the wake of my financial downfall, I accumulated significant credit card debt, and it took me a long time to get out of it. Though I'd dramatically changed my relationship with money, I was on my own. I didn't have sufficient support, guidance, or accountability in place, and I thought I had changed patterns more than I actually had. So once again, I got into credit card debt.

I had repeated this cycle many times in the past, but this time it was different. I had accumulated some debt, but I was still meeting my obligations and making payments on time. I wasn't avoiding my bills, and I was present with the situation up to a point—but I had overestimated my ability to handle credit. That was because I hadn't been paying close attention to the impact of my decisions; I had made improvements, but I wasn't there yet. I had another level of mastery to aim for.

Because I had cultivated awareness and made some significant changes in my behavior, I was able to recover from this temporary backslide. I had wandered off course, but was able to get back on track. This wouldn't have been the case if I hadn't been continuing my Spiritual Finance journey. It was a tough lesson to learn, but it taught me to be cautious when making spending decisions. I now respect money in a way I wouldn't have otherwise.

Maintaining this degree of watchfulness has sometimes been frustrating. At times I would become impatient with the slow process of correcting my money cycles and the inevitable failures along the way, but when I maintained a long view, I could see significant progress. Because I'd had so many bad habits in the past, being overly diligent for a while was insurance that I wouldn't fall into the same patterns again.

It's like a pendulum swing. At one end of the pendulum swing is my past, when I was unaware of my relationship with money and fueled by fear, assumptions, limiting beliefs, and habitual cycles. On the other end of the pendulum swing is a relationship with money that is overly rigid, cautious, and disciplined. Things have relaxed as I've created a new cycle in my relationship with money, and gradually I've come to a more balanced and relaxed place, which is closer to the center point of the pendulum swing.

The lesson is to remain aware of our cycles with money. Old habits can take time to change, and it is a worthwhile investment of time and energy to stay diligent, with support and accountability, to create a healthy and sustainable new cycle.

Conclusion

Creating a healthy relationship with money—one that is consciously aligned with your values—is a process. It requires you to become your most fascinating research project, one that begins with understanding where you are now and how you got here. Your history created this reality, but it doesn't have to dictate your future.

Developing a new relationship with money requires courage, patience, perseverance, and the willingness to challenge your assumptions—to confront your patterns, habits, and limiting beliefs. Feeling awkward at first is a natural consequence of learning and an indication that you're doing something new.

Over time, you will make progress. It may initially seem imperceptible, but every small step you make—in thinking, attitude, expectations, beliefs, or behavior — adds up, and will take you somewhere. By navigating with clarity and purpose, you will shift things.

When you plant a seed, at first you don't see any change. Gazing at the soil, you question whether anything is happening. Yet all the while, beneath the surface, there is activity. Each seed grows in its own way, according to its individual dictates, and so do people. This process will look different for each person, and at first it may not seem like things are changing. But rest assured that change, even if it feels invisible at the moment, is happening. Trust, faith, and patience will serve you well, and sooner than you expect, you will be able to look back and see the progress you're making.

To create lasting, sustainable change, you must remain engaged and present. Practice new ways of thinking about and acting with money. Develop new habits and remain flexible as you grow. Your relationship with money is constantly evolving, and you will be required to respond to changing conditions. Going it alone is not impossible, but will likely be more difficult and take more time. Be brave! Talk about money. You'll find that you have more in common with other people than you ever imagined, and their support will ease the way.

Structured accountability is an investment that will pay off, literally and figuratively.

By changing your relationship with money, you will influence the people around you. You will model a new reality and prove that change is possible: If you can do it, so can others. By changing your own relationship with money, you will influence the world around you as we change our collective relationship with money.

Recommended Reading

Countless books have been written about money. I recommend the ones below to participants in the Spiritual Finance class series because they have specifically informed my journey.

The Four Spiritual Laws of Prosperity
   by Edwene Gaines

It's Not About the Money by Brent Kessel

Secrets of the Millionaire Mind by T. Harv Eker

The Soul of Money by Lynne Twist

Spiritual Finance
Changing our individual and collective relationship with money …

Since 2008, Kerry Cudmore has taught her Spiritual Finance class series to hundreds of people, helping them redesign their core relationship with money. Devoted to eliminating the suffering that can be connected to money, she works with individuals, businesses, and organizations to permanently shift the financial atmosphere of our culture.

If you are interested in learning more about Spiritual Finance, please visit: kerrycudmore.com

Acknowledgement

I have been helped in many ways by many people. My gratitude could go on for days.

For everyone who has allowed me to witness their journey through the Spiritual Finance process; I am sincerely grateful. You prove that changing our individual and collective relationship with money is possible — and can be a lot of fun in the process.

To the Spiritual Finance Advanced Community members throughout the years; thank you for your authentic presence and courage. You prove that expansion in life, and in relationship with money, is more than a possibility — it is an enlightenment.

My gratitude could go on for days, and will continue for a few more pages ...

Jim St. Pierre; you believed in me even when I refused to, and helped me even when I didn't believe I deserved it. You've selflessly held me up time and time again, and I pinch myself that you're in my life. *I am grateful.* Cameron McCarthy; you are the best example of what this book hopes to inspire. As I witness your relationship with money I am awed by your thinking and behavior. Your kind-hearted nature, authenticity, humor, and willingness to put up with a bit of an odd Mom helps me every day. *I am grateful.* Edwene Gaines; you gave me tithing, and the courage to begin this sacred practice for myself. It was an answer to my quest. *I am grateful.* Edward Espe Brown; your presence in my life has shone a light for me. I look to you time and again, as confirmation that generous authentic expression is truly the way. *I am grateful.* Tolly Burkan; your uncensored oomph gives me courage, and lends me belief in the grace of my intrinsic Self. *I am grateful.*

Octopus Leadership Tribe; though we are far-flung, various, and as wonky as our name implies, you were my catalyst and remain a constant touchstone. *I am grateful.* Thursday Theology Group; precious gems—your friendship is invaluable. *I am grateful.* My clients; without you I wouldn't have this life I love. Your support, and the way you show up to our work together, keep me constantly inspired and engaged. *I am grateful.* Bob D'Amico; you talked me down from my financial ledge without judgement, and with consummate wit, intelligence, honesty, and patience. You made being present with money safe and approachable, and helped me face my reality so that I could change it. *I am grateful.* Barbara Nordin; I'm delighted to have found you. Your unwavering positive belief and mentorship helped make this book a reality. *I am grateful.* Whoever is reading this right now; thank you! *I am grateful for you too …*

Kerry Cudmore is a professional certified life and business coach, empowerment trainer, and firewalking instructor who has made a lifetime study of human expression. She creates and teaches methods that make complex concepts easy to understand and master so that clients and class participants can create joyful, prosperous, and fulfilling lives and businesses. She is founder of the Spiritual Finance Initiative, which is devoted to changing our individual and collective relationships with money.

Kerry lives in Westport Massachusetts, where she simultaneously annoys and amuses her fiancé and son while watching cow TV, conducting experiments in ridiculous gardening, and listening to the parrot repeat everything she wished she hadn't said … in her own voice.